DREW BREES
and the
New Orleans Saints

SUPER BOWL XLIV

by Michael Sandler

Consultant: Norries Wilson
Head Football Coach
Columbia University

BEARPORT
PUBLISHING

New York, New York

Credits

Cover and Title Page, © Andy Lyons/Getty Images; 4, © AP Images/Mike Groll; 5, © Andy Lyons/Getty Images; 6, © Austin American-Statesman/WPN; 7, © Austin American-Statesman/WPN; 8, © Donald Miralle/Allsport/Getty Images; 9, © Kevin Reece/Icon SMI/Newscom; 10, © AP Images/Eric Gay; 11, © AP Images/ Bill Haber; 12, © Dan Anderson/epa/Corbis; 13, © Larry French/Getty Images; 14, © AP Images/David J. Phillip; 15, © AP Images/Kevin Terrell; 16, © Rhona Wise/ epa/Corbis; 17, © AP Images/Rob Carr; 18, © Timothy A. Clary/AFP/Newscom; 19, © John G. Mabanglo/epa/Corbis; 20, © Charles Trainor Jr./Miami Herald/ MCT/Newscom; 21, © Tom Fox/Dallas Morning News/MCT/Newscom; 22L, © Todd Kirkland/Icon SMI/Newscom; 22R, © AP Photo/David Stluka; 22 Background, © Timothy A. Clary/AFP/Newscom.

Publisher: Kenn Goin
Senior Editor: Lisa Wiseman
Creative Director: Spencer Brinker
Design: Debrah Kaiser
Photo Researcher: Picture Perfect Professionals, LLC

Library of Congress Cataloging-in-Publication Data

Sandler, Michael.
  Drew Brees and the New Orleans Saints : Super Bowl xliv / by Michael Sandler.
     p. cm. — (Super bowl superstars)
  Includes bibliographical references and index.
  ISBN-13: 978-1-936088-27-0 (library binding)
  ISBN-10: 1-936088-27-4 (library binding)
  1. Brees, Drew, 1979—Juvenile literature. 2. Football players—United States— Biography—Juvenile literature. 3. Quarterbacks (Football) —United States— Biography—Juvenile literature. 4. New Orleans Saints (Football team) —Juvenile literature. 5. Super Bowl—Juvenile literature. I. Title.
  GV939.B695S36 2011
  796.332092—dc22
  (B)

                        2010009581

For more information, write to Bearport Publishing Company, Inc., 101 Fifth Avenue, Suite 6R, New York, New York 10003. Printed in the United States of America in North Mankato, Minnesota.

062010
042110CGC

10 9 8 7 6 5 4 3 2 1

★ Contents ★

Falling Behind

Things were looking pretty grim for the New Orleans Saints. The first quarter of Super Bowl XLIV (44) wasn't even over, and already the Indianapolis Colts had a ten-point lead.

Saints fans were worried. The Colts and their incredible quarterback Peyton Manning looked unstoppable, and history wasn't on New Orleans's side. Only one team had ever come back to win the Super Bowl after falling so far behind.

Still, Saints quarterback Drew Brees remained calm. He loved challenges—the bigger, the better. To Drew, there was nothing better than being an **underdog**.

A touchdown pass from Colts quarterback Peyton Manning to Pierre Garcon (#85) put Indianapolis ahead, 10-0.

Drew Brees during
Super Bowl XLIV (44)

In 1988, after being
down ten points in Super Bowl
XXII (22), the Washington
Redskins were able to come
back and defeat the Denver
Broncos, 42-10.

5

Enjoying Challenges

Growing up in Austin, Texas, Drew had loved the underdog role. When kids chose sides for schoolyard sports, he preferred to end up on the weaker team. "To him, it meant a lot more to win when you weren't supposed to," remembers Tom Costas, his middle school **flag football** coach.

Drew was such a strong athlete that his teams usually won no matter who his teammates were. By high school, the talented teen was excelling in three sports: baseball, basketball, and, of course, football. With Drew as the starting quarterback, the football team won 28 games without a single loss.

Drew at a Westlake High School football practice

In his senior year, Drew and his Westlake High School teammates won the Texas State Football Championship.

Drew on the field during a game in which Westlake won, 55-15

A Little Short

Drew found that he was still an underdog when it came time to choose a college in 1997. Normally, Texas champion quarterbacks draw a lot of attention from big football schools. Drew, however, received just two **scholarship** offers. The main reason was his height. Football coaches liked tall quarterbacks, and Drew was barely six feet (1.83 m) tall.

With limited choices, Drew chose Purdue University, a school not known for a great football program. There, however, he became one of the nation's best college quarterbacks. After graduation, Drew was selected by the San Diego Chargers in the 2001 NFL **draft**.

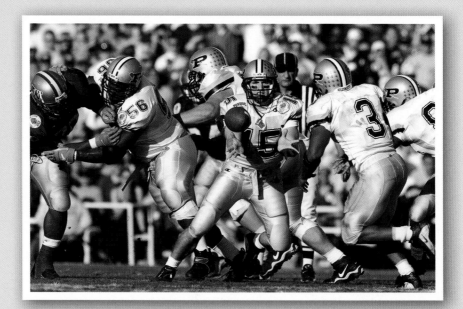

Drew (#15) throws the ball to a Purdue teammate during the Rose Ball in 2001.

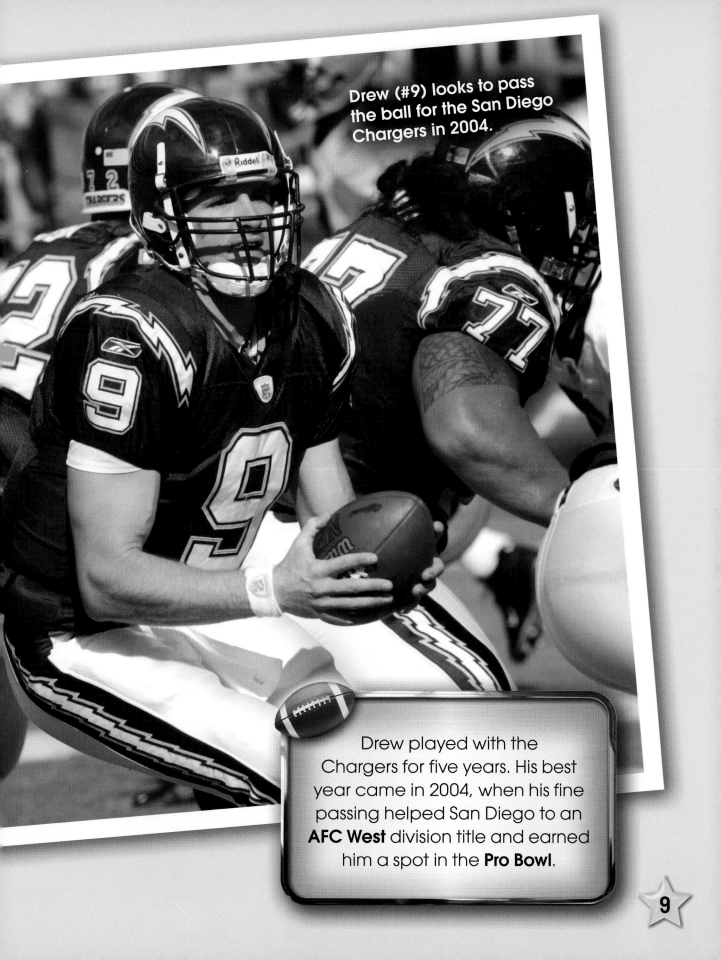

Drew (#9) looks to pass the ball for the San Diego Chargers in 2004.

Drew played with the Chargers for five years. His best year came in 2004, when his fine passing helped San Diego to an **AFC West** division title and earned him a spot in the **Pro Bowl**.

The City of New Orleans

Drew joined the New Orleans Saints as a **free agent** in 2006. He was moving to a city that was struggling to survive. A year earlier, **Hurricane Katrina** had struck New Orleans, flooding and destroying homes, and killing more than 1,000 people.

New Orleans coach Sean Payton drove Drew through the city's ruined neighborhoods. It looked to Drew as if a nuclear bomb had gone off. Stunned, Drew decided he wasn't just going to be the Saints' quarterback. As a New Orleans resident, he was going to do everything he could to help rebuild the city.

Even the Superdome, where the New Orleans Saints play, was completely flooded by Hurricane Katrina.

Here, Drew helps rebuild a home that was destroyed by the hurricane.

Since joining the Saints, Drew has helped raise millions of dollars to rebuild homes, schools, and parks damaged by the storm and to support programs for the children of New Orleans.

Turning the Saints Around

The Saints, like the city of New Orleans, were in need of some rebuilding, too. The team had enjoyed little success in more than 40 years of NFL play. The year before Drew joined, the team won only three games.

Drew worked hard to turn the team around. In his very first season, New Orleans made it all the way into the **NFC Championship Game**.

Even more success came in 2009. The Saints won their first 13 games as they made their way to the playoffs. After huge playoff wins over the Arizona Cardinals and the Minnesota Vikings, the New Orleans Saints headed to the Super Bowl.

Coach Sean Payton (right) and Drew (left) talk during the game against the Minnesota Vikings.

Drew (#9) gets ready to throw the ball during the Saints' 31-28 victory over the Vikings.

Before the 2009 season, the Saints had never played in a single Super Bowl.

13

Peyton and the Colts

In Super Bowl XLIV (44), New Orleans was facing an extremely tough opponent. The Indianapolis Colts had the NFL's best record and football's most feared quarterback—Peyton Manning.

Peyton had already won Super Bowl XLI (41) and was often called the best quarterback in NFL history. His Colts had little trouble defeating the Baltimore Ravens and the New York Jets in the playoffs on the way to the Super Bowl. Although many people were rooting for Drew and the Saints, few fans gave them much chance of defeating Peyton and the Colts.

Peyton Manning talks to reporters before Super Bowl XLIV (44).

Peyton Manning looks to pass the ball during the playoff game against the New York Jets in January 2010. The Colts won the game, 30-17.

Since joining Indianapolis in 1998, Peyton has started in every game his team has played—that's 192 games in a row. He has also been named an NFL **MVP** four times, more than any other player.

A Bad Beginning

Early in Super Bowl XLIV (44), Drew and the Saints seemed shaky. On one play, Drew **overthrew wide receiver** Robert Meachem. On another, Saints receiver Marques Colston dropped an easy pass. Peyton and the Colts, on the other hand, looked great as they quickly ran out to a 10-0 first quarter lead.

Despite his early troubles, Drew stayed calm. The tough Colts' **defense** didn't allow him to throw long passes, so Drew made short ones. He was eventually able to lead the Saints on two long **drives** made up of many short plays. New Orleans soon cut the Indianapolis lead to 10-6 with two field goals.

Drew (#9) hands off the ball to running back Pierre Thomas (#23).

New Orleans Saints wide receiver Devery Henderson (#19) leaps in the air to catch a pass.

During the second quarter, Drew kept his **offense** on the field for all but two minutes of play. That meant that Peyton Manning was mostly off the field, unable to score points for the Colts.

Duel of the Quarterbacks

When the second half began, Coach Payton made a gutsy call. He had the Saints' kicker try an onside kick. If it didn't work, the Colts would get the ball in New Orleans territory and have a great chance to score. Fortunately, the gamble paid off—the Saints recovered the ball.

Drew quickly found running back Pierre Thomas for a touchdown pass, giving the Saints a 13-10 lead. Peyton responded with his own touchdown drive to put the Colts ahead, 17-13. Drew then led his team into **field goal range**. Garrett Hartley's perfect kick made the score 17-16. Both quarterbacks were putting on a show. Who would win—Drew the underdog or Peyton the superstar?

Both teams scrambled for the ball after the onside kick.

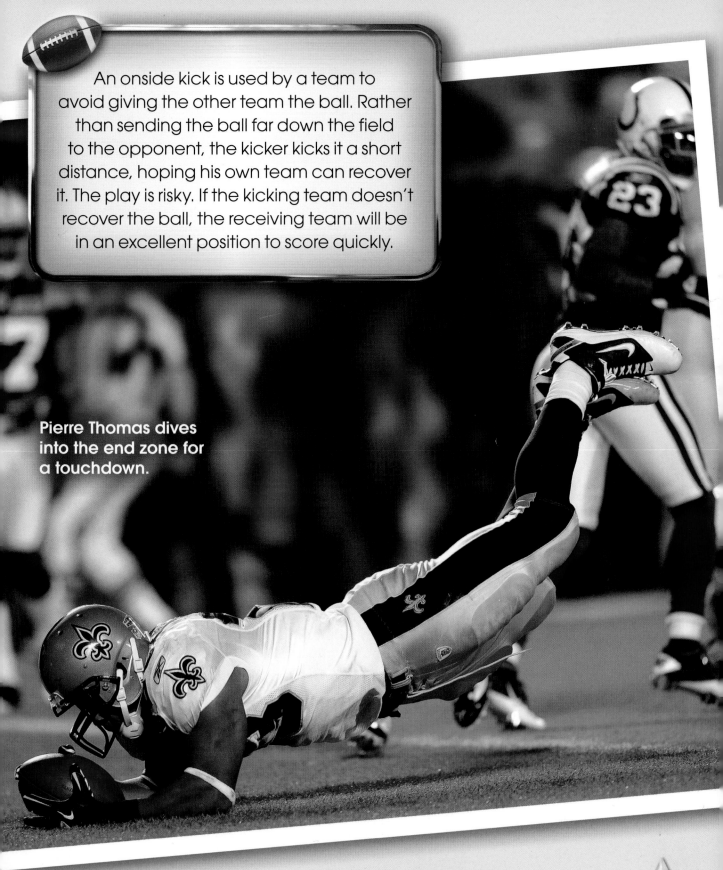

An onside kick is used by a team to avoid giving the other team the ball. Rather than sending the ball far down the field to the opponent, the kicker kicks it a short distance, hoping his own team can recover it. The play is risky. If the kicking team doesn't recover the ball, the receiving team will be in an excellent position to score quickly.

Pierre Thomas dives into the end zone for a touchdown.

The Saints March to Victory

In the end, Drew outplayed Peyton. He threw crisp passes to six different receivers on a 59-yard (54-m) touchdown drive. New Orleans led, 24-17!

Peyton, master of last-second comebacks, had one more chance. He brought his team deep into New Orleans territory. Then, with three minutes left to play, Saints **cornerback** Tracy Porter darted in front of Colts receiver Reggie Wayne. Tracy **intercepted** Peyton's throw and ran all the way into the **end zone**. The 74-yard (68-m) touchdown sealed the win for the Saints. The city of New Orleans had its first Super Bowl title!

Tracy Porter's interception return gave New Orleans a 31-17 win.

After the game, Drew said, "This championship is for you, New Orleans."

With 32 completions in 39 attempts, 288 passing yards (263 m), and two touchdowns, Drew's performance was one of the greatest in Super Bowl history. He was named MVP of Super Bowl XLIV (44).

There were other key players on the New Orleans Saints who helped win Super Bowl XLIV (44). Here are two of them.

Pierre Thomas #23

Position: Running Back

Born: 12/18/1984 in Chicago, Illinois

Height: 5' 11" (1.80 m)

Weight: 215 pounds (98 kg)

Key Plays: Gained 85 yards (78 m) rushing and receiving; caught a 16-yard (15-m) touchdown pass in the third quarter to give the Saints their first lead

Tracy Porter #22

Position: Cornerback

Born: 8/11/1986 in Port Allen, Louisiana

Height: 5' 11" (1.80 m)

Weight: 186 pounds (84 kg)

Key Play: Intercepted a fourth-quarter pass by Peyton Manning and returned it 74 yards (68 m) for a touchdown

★ Glossary ★

AFC West (AY-EFF-SEE WEST) one of the four divisions in the NFL's American Football Conference (AFC)

cornerback (KOR-nur-bak) a player on defense who usually covers the other team's receivers

defense (DEE-fenss) the part of a team that has the job of stopping the other team from scoring

draft (DRAFT) an event in which professional teams take turns choosing college players to play for them

drives (DRIVEZ) a series of plays that begin when a team gets the ball; the plays end when the team with the ball either scores or gives up the ball to the other team

end zone (END ZOHN) the area at either end of a football field where touchdowns are scored

field goal range (FEELD GOHL RAYNJ) the area of the field where a kicker is close enough to be able to make a field goal

flag football (FLAG FUT-*bal*) a version of football in which players are not tackled; instead, defenders end a play by removing a flag worn by the ball carrier

free agent (FREE AY-juhnt) a player who is not signed to a team and can choose which team to play for

Hurricane Katrina (HUR-uh-*kane* kuh-TREE-nuh) a massive storm that caused incredible destruction in New Orleans and on the surrounding coast in late August 2005

intercepted (*in*-tur-SEP-tid) caught a pass meant for a player on the other team

MVP (EM-VEE-PEE) the most valuable player

NFC Championship Game (EN-EFF-SEE CHAM-pee-uhn-*ship* GAME) a playoff game that determines which National Football Conference (NFC) team will go to the Super Bowl

offense (AW-fenss) the part of a team that has the job of scoring

overthrew (*oh*-vur-THROO) threw a ball too far for the receiver to catch

Pro Bowl (PROH BOHL) the yearly All-Star game for the season's best NFL players

scholarship (SKOL-ur-ship) an award that helps pay for a person to go to college

underdog (UHN-dur-*dawg*) an athlete who is not expected to win

wide receiver (WIDE ri-SEE-vur) a player whose job it is to catch passes

Bibliography

Battista, Judy. "Saints' Brees Debunks Notions of the Quarterback Prototype." *The New York Times* (November 29, 2009).

Orsborn, Tom. "Saints Star Brees Thrives as an Underdog." *San Antonio Express News* (January 31, 2010).

The Indianapolis Star

The Times-Picayune (New Orleans)

NFL.com

Read More

Gilbert, Sara. *The Story of the New Orleans Saints (The NFL Today)*. Mankato, MN: Creative Education (2009).

Sandler, Michael. *Peyton Manning and the Indianapolis Colts: Super Bowl XLI (Super Bowl Superstars)*. New York: Bearport (2008).

Sandler, Michael. *Pro Football's Dream Teams (Football-O-Rama)*. New York: Bearport (2011).

Sandler, Michael. *Pro Football's Most Spectacular Quarterbacks (Football-O-Rama)*. New York: Bearport (2011).

Learn More Online

To learn more about Drew Brees,
the New Orleans Saints, and the Super Bowl, visit
www.bearportpublishing.com/SuperBowlSuperstars

Index